ECO STEAM

the CITIES WE LIVE IN

GEORGIA AMSON-BRADSHAW

WAYLAND
www.waylandbooks.co.uk

First published in Great Britain in 2018 by Wayland

Produced for Wayland by
White-Thomson Publishing Ltd
www.wtpub.co.uk

Series Editor: Georgia Amson-Bradshaw
Series Designer: Rocket Design (East Anglia) Ltd

ISBN: 978 1 5263 0788 0
10 9 8 7 6 5 4 3 2 1

MIX
Paper from responsible sources
FSC® C104740

Wayland
An imprint of
Hachette Children's Group
Part of Hodder & Stoughton
Carmelite House
50 Victoria Embankment
London EC4Y 0DZ

An Hachette UK Company
www.hachette.co.uk
www.hachettechildrens.co.uk

Printed in China

Picture acknowledgements:
Images from Shutterstock: nuttavut sammongkol 4t, f11photo 5t, Bluehousestudio 5c, Marina Poushkina 5b, Hung Chung Chih 6t, Pavel Chagochkin 6c, Iconic Bestiary 6br, Danila Shtantsov 7b, Trekandshoot 9t, Mascha Tace 9c, Huza 9bl, Boo-Tique 10t, alice-photo 10b, I Wei Huang 11t, Logoboom 11c, Rawmn 11br, SAPhotog 11bl, WINS86 13t, CreatOR76 14br, Petovarga 14-15b, Lgogosha 16bl, Fancy Tapis 17t, jkcDesign 17c, TWStock 17b, SERASOOT 18t, Pixelrain 19t, Faber14 20t, Equinoxvert 20bl, mubus7 20br, Jeiel Shamblee 21b, Andrew Babble 24b,Kalinin Ilya 25t, Macrovector 25b, Africa Studio 26c, KONGKY 27t, Macrovector 27c, Connel 27br, Vladwel 28t, Kiberstalker 28b, ProStockStudio 29c, Icon Bunny 30br, Bioraven 31cl, EpicStockMedia 32t, VladimirCeresnak 32b, Iva Villi 33t, PODIS 33c, NASA Images 33b, Diyana Dimitrova 34t, amperespy44 34b, MilanB 35tl, Wectors 35tr, Mahesh Patil 35c, Colorcocktail 35bl, Kraska 35br, Natykach Nataliia 36t, d1sk 36b, mejnak 37t, hexeparu 37b, RedlineVector 38br, Studio64 40t, Avian 40b, Papajka 41t, 24Novembers 41c, Mopic 41b, tele52 42tl and 42br, Sunflowerey 43t, stocker1970 43c, Sean Pavone 43b, DUSIT PAICHALERM 44t, Rido 46t, Miiisha 46br, nelya43 48b

Images from Wikimedia Commons: Soman 8r, Mario Roberto Duran Ortiz Mariordo 44b
Illustrations by Steve Evans 30bl, 39b
All design elements from Shutterstock.

CONTENTS

CITY LIFE

Do you live in an urban area such as a city or town, or in the countryside? Around the world, over 50 per cent of us live in urban areas. This is more than ever before, and this proportion is predicted to go up to around 70 per cent by the year 2050. Human beings live increasingly urban lives, and this greatly affects how we interact with the natural world and our impact on it.

Security and opportunity

People often move to cities in search of better job opportunities and living standards. In many countries, people in rural areas depend on the food they can grow for themselves. In this situation, even low-paid jobs and cramped living conditions in the city can offer more security than living off the land. Climate change, the human-influenced disturbance of natural weather patterns, has already affected places such as the Sahel in Africa, where drought has made farming very difficult for rural people.

Land suffering from drought in Ethiopia

SPOTLIGHT:

URBANISATION

The trend of people moving from rural areas to cities is called urbanisation. Many of the world's poorer countries are experiencing rapid urbanisation at the moment.

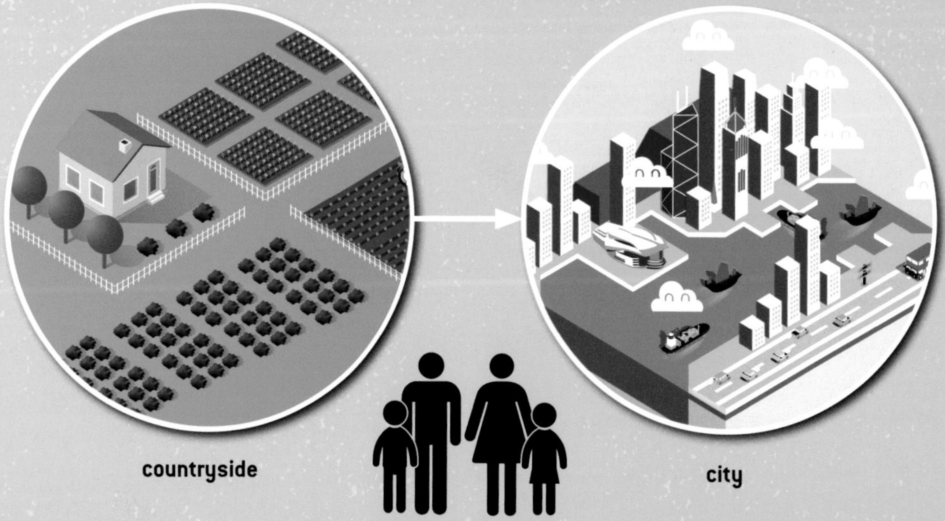

Megacities

As the global human population has grown, and more and more people have moved to urban areas, the size of our cities has greatly increased. In 1950 there were only two cities in the world with more than 10 million inhabitants (called megacities). By 2017, that number was 47.

Tokyo is the largest city in the world, with **38 MILLION** inhabitants.

Future cities

Areas of the world are urbanising fast, and new cities can spring up over the course of only a couple of decades. This is both an opportunity and a challenge when it comes to making sure our cities are sustainable (meaning they don't negatively affect the environment). Building new cities gives us opportunities to use the most up-to-date, eco-friendly technology – but fast, unplanned and unlimited development can seriously damage the natural environment.

CHANGING CITIES

Urban areas are responsible for 70 per cent of energy use and carbon dioxide emissions. The good news is that the nature of cities means that they have the potential to become sustainable very fast.

Fumes from traffic and power plants cause air pollution in Beijing, China.

Building modern, eco-friendly public transport networks can reduce cities' impact on the climate.

SPOTLIGHT:

CARBON DIOXIDE EMISSIONS

Carbon dioxide (CO_2) is a greenhouse gas, meaning that it traps heat from the Sun in our atmosphere, causing the Earth to heat up. Emissions are releases of gas during the burning of fuel or processing of chemicals.

Centres of change

Cities are dynamic places, and their inhabitants can adapt quickly to change. Because cities contain so many people, when new technologies such as eco-friendly transport are put in place they can have a really big impact right away.

Climate change danger

Cities contribute a lot to climate change due to the high use of energy and resources by the people who live in them. But at the same time many cities are at high risk from the effects of climate change. Many cities, including some of the world's largest, are built on the coast. This puts them at risk of flooding as sea levels rise. Millions of people around the world could be forced to move as the effects of climate change become more severe.

Cities including Shanghai, Mumbai and New York, are at risk of flooding from sea level rises due to climate change.

Old cities and new

Politicians, developers, scientists and citizens around the world are working on ways to make new and existing cities more sustainable. The technologies used will differ depending on how established each city is, and the local climate and landscape. In this book, you'll discover some ways to create eco-friendly cities using science, technology, engineering, design and maths.

Trees line the roads to help clean the air in Singapore.

THE ISSUE:

URBAN SPRAWL

How close do you live to your neighbours? If you live in a block of flats, they are very close by. If you live on a farm in the countryside, you might not even be able to see your neighbours' house. Can you walk to the nearest shop, or would you have to go by car or bus? The answers to these questions tell you about the density of where you live.

Dhaka in Bangladesh is the world's most densely populated city, with

44,500

people per square kilometre.

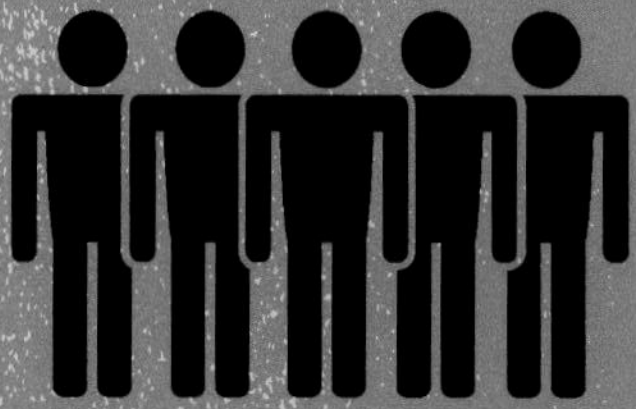

Density and sprawl

People aren't evenly spread around the country; some areas have more people living there than others. 'Population density' describes how many people live in a certain place. Cities have denser populations than the countryside, but even within cities there are areas of different density. Inner-city areas usually have the highest density, with lots of people living in flats, and a mixture of shops and workplaces near by. As cities expand outwards into previously rural areas, they tend to get less dense. This is often referred to as urban sprawl, and it can cause problems for people and the environment.

Car dependency

Areas of urban sprawl on the outer edges of cities tend to have larger houses and fewer shops and workplaces. These areas often have limited public transport, meaning the people who live there may be completely car-dependent, having to drive to access the basic necessities of life such as buying food and going to school or work.

Fossil fuel use

Being reliant on cars creates big environmental problems (read more about this on pages 24–31). Cars burn fossil fuels, releasing greenhouse gases into the atmosphere and contributing to climate change. They also pollute the air, with negative effects on people's health, such as lung disease.

Human impacts

Areas of low-density housing without shops, schools and other meeting places such as community centres can affect people's physical and mental health. Being dependent on cars means people walk less, making them less healthy. Without community meeting spaces that allow people to regularly interact with their neighbours, people can become isolated and lonely.

Habitat loss

Urban sprawl impacts on wildlife by causing habitat loss. As natural areas are paved over, the homes of animals, birds and insects are destroyed.

URBAN LAND USE

A very old town that starts out as a small settlement of just a few hundred people can sometimes grow into a city with many thousands or millions of inhabitants. As the city expands, the way the land is used changes. More land is given over to housing, factories, shops and offices. Often, different types of land use become grouped together in zones.

Concentric circles

A very simple diagram of land use that can be found in some cities and towns is called the Concentric, or Burgess Model. The oldest parts of the city are usually in the centre, and the more recently built parts are on the outside.

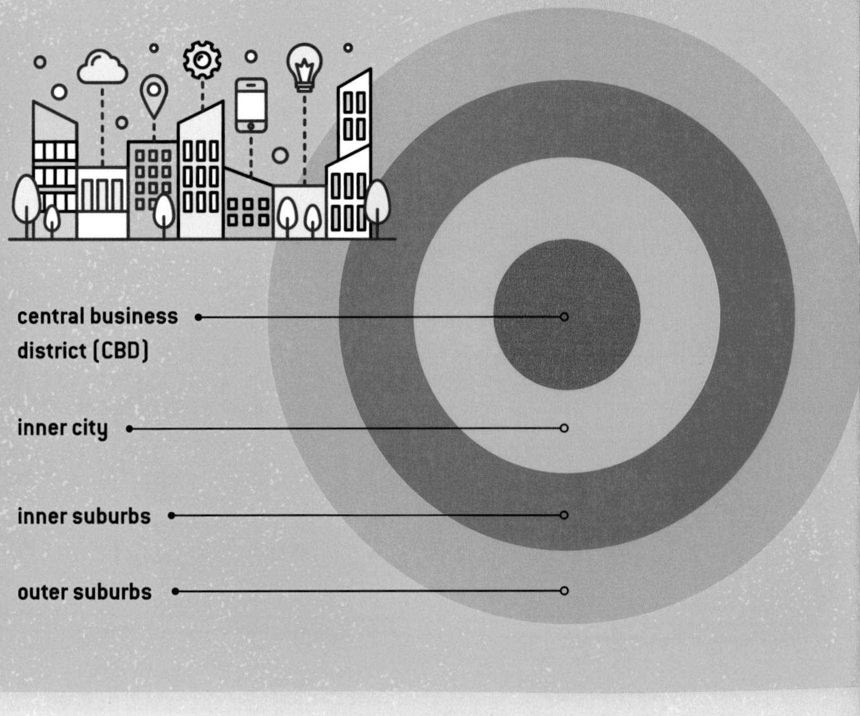

CDB

The very centre is called the central business district, or CBD. It contains businesses, shops and offices, and many transport routes such as railway lines lead there.

Inner city

Historically, the inner city contained factories and housing for the workers. The housing was tightly packed so that many people could live in the area and walk to work. Today these areas tend not to contain factories, but a high-density mixture of types of land use. Housing often is within high-rise flats, and there are many shops, cafés and other businesses and public spaces.

Inner suburbs

When cities grew outwards in the twentieth century, suburbs began to be built that either took advantage of transport links such as railways or made use of the growing popularity of the car. These areas are less dense. Many of the houses are semi-detached and have individual gardens.

Outer suburbs

The zone at the edge of the city tends to be the least dense, with more detached housing and housing estates. Shops and offices tend to be clustered in large retail or industrial parks that are only accessible by car.

SPOTLIGHT: GREEN BELT

A green belt is an area of land around a city where building is not allowed. This is to try and prevent urban sprawl.

SOLVE IT!
SUSTAINABLE CITY PLANNING

Large areas of unsustainable urban sprawl are not good for people or the planet. However, as more people move to cities, new housing, shops and transport infrastructure need to be built to accommodate them. How should new city developments be designed?

HOUSING

What style of housing should be built and why?

single family home

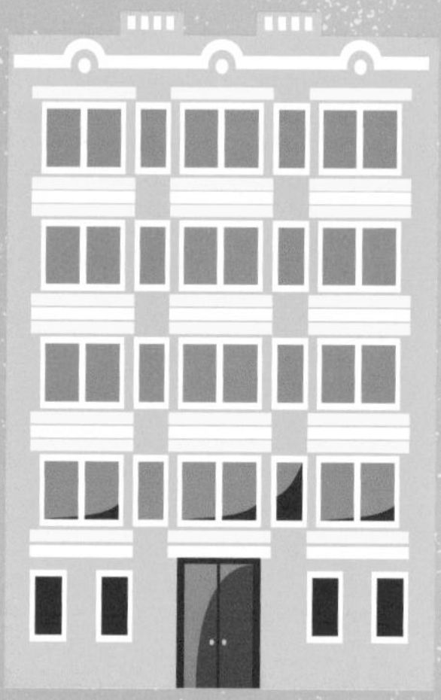

apartment building

TRANSPORT

How should residents of the city get around? What sort of city layout would help them to use sustainable methods of transport?

FACILITIES

Where should facilities such as schools, shops, doctors' clinics and libraries be placed in relation to the housing?

school

library

hospital

supermarket

BIRD'S-EYE VIEW

Get a piece of plain or squared paper and some drawing materials. Try designing some maps of city layouts that you think are more sustainable.

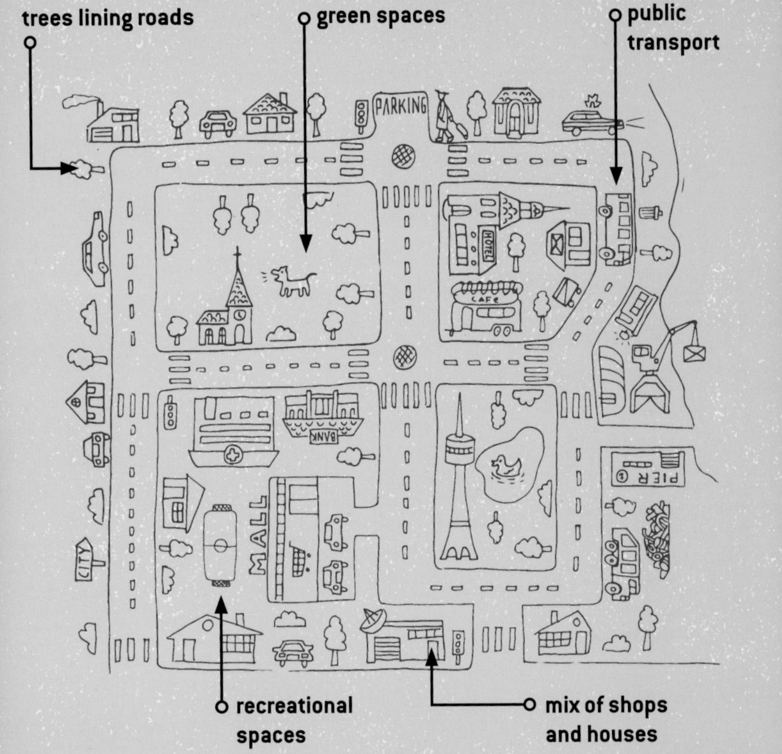

STREET VIEW

Draw a picture of what a typical street might look like in your sustainably designed city.

CAN YOU SOLVE IT?

Once you have thought about all these elements, and have drawn a layout you are happy with and illustrated a picture of a typical street, why not stick them on some card and add labels to create a display explaining your vision?

Still need some inspiration? See page 42 for some ideas.

TEST IT!
LAND USE PROJECT

Study the land use in your own neighbourhood with this project, and see how it compares to another area in your town or city.

YOU WILL NEED

- a computer with internet
- a printer
- a pencil
- colouring pencils in three colours
- paper
- a ruler
- a calculator

WARNING: Don't go anywhere without an adult.

STEP 1

Decide which areas you want to study. Perhaps your own street, and another in your local town that you can visit? In order to make a fair comparison between two areas you'll need to ensure they are the same size, for example you might choose two 500-metre-long stretches of road.

STEP 2

Go to Google Maps and find your first chosen area. Zoom in until you can see the outlines of the buildings. Print out the map showing your 500-metre stretch.

STEP 3

Walk along your chosen stretch. Look at each building. Is it residential (e.g. a house), non-residential (e.g. an office) or a mix (e.g. a shop with flats on top). Choose a different colour to represent each of these three types, and colour in the buildings on your printout to show how each is being used.

STEP 4

As well as identifying the type of land use for each building, count up how many residential and non-residential units there are along your stretch. So for example, a detached house is one unit, but a block of flats might contain many units. It won't always be obvious from the building type, so try counting doorbells to get a rough number!

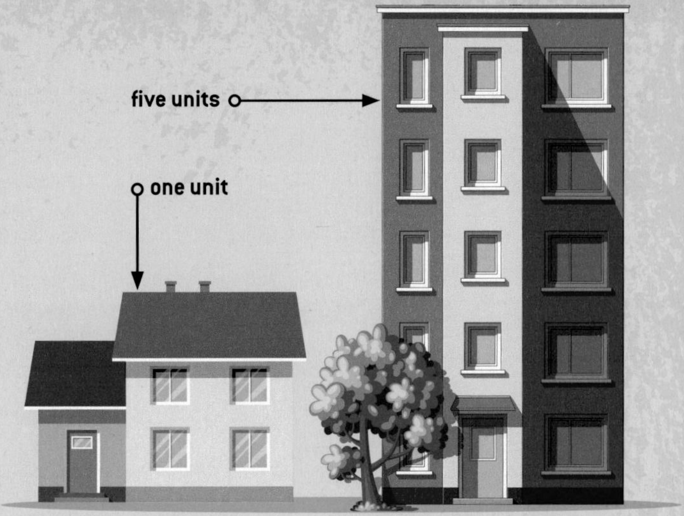

STEP 5

Repeat these two surveys for the second area of the same size in your town. Aim to choose a different type of area, so if you live on the outskirts of a town, try repeating it in the city centre.

STEP 6

Count up the number of residential, non-residential and mixed-use buildings in each of your areas. Calculate the percentage of each type for both areas. Draw a bar chart or two pie charts to show your results side by side.

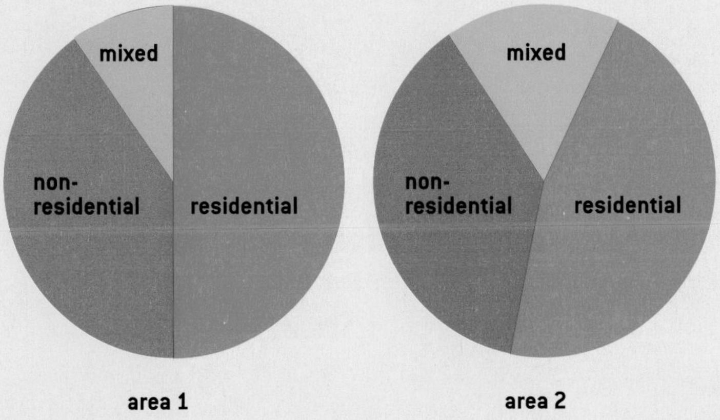

STEP 7

Compare the number of units of each type in your two areas. Which has a higher density of units?

THE ISSUE:

LACK OF GREEN SPACE

Picture a city scene in your head. What colours can you see in your mind's eye? Grey buildings and roads? Some brightly coloured billboards or shop signs? You probably don't picture many green plants. One problem related to urban sprawl and urban land use can be the lack of green space within cities. And, like urban sprawl, this has negative impacts on both humans and wildlife – sometimes in surprising ways.

Habitat fragmentation

As well as habitat loss, urban expansion can cause the related problem of habitat fragmentation. Animals need to move around to find food and mates, and to avoid competition. But when areas of habitat are broken up by large paved areas, it can prevent them from being able to move from place to place.

Mental health

We don't often think of it, but human beings are animals too! Studies have shown that access to nature and to green spaces is very good for our well-being and mental health. People who spend time in green spaces are happier and less stressed. Access to these areas, such as parks, is good for physical health too, as people are encouraged to get more exercise through play, walking and cycling.

Hospital patients who can see greenery through a window get better faster.

Urban heat island

All the dark-coloured and paved surfaces in a city create a surprising phenomenon, called the 'heat island effect'. Dark, hard surfaces, such as tarmac and concrete, store heat from the Sun and release it at night. This makes cities several degrees hotter than the surrounding countryside.

In the USA, around 1,000 people die from extreme heat each year.

Dangerous temperatures

The heat island effect can be a particular problem in hot countries, where temperatures in cities can become dangerous for residents. People can die during heatwaves in hot regions, where temperatures are made even more deadly by the heat island effect. The additional heat, along with city air pollution, can create a special type of air pollution called ground-level ozone, which can damage people's lungs.

HEATING AND COOLING

Urban heat islands are created by large areas of dark, artificial surfaces and a lack of greenery such as trees, shrubs and other plants. But how are the respective heating and cooling effects produced?

OUCH!

Dark surfaces can get very hot from the Sun's heat.

Light and dark surfaces

Have you ever walked barefoot on dark-coloured tarmac on a sunny day? It was probably very hot. Now think about white plastic garden furniture that gets left outside – does that ever get as hot? White or light-coloured surfaces reflect more heat and light than dark-coloured surfaces. This is called the albedo effect. Dark surfaces absorb the heat, and then slowly give it off. This is how the dark surfaces of cities create the urban heat island effect (see page 17).

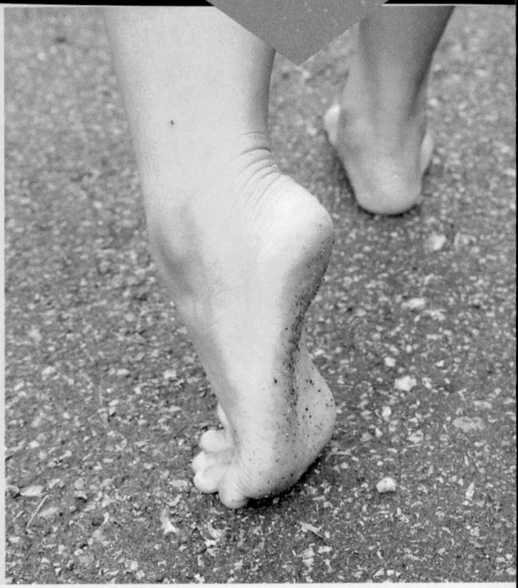

Green leaves on plants and other trees are a lighter colour than tarmac, and so reflect more of the Sun's heat.

Evaporative cooling

Think what happens when you get hot – you sweat! Humans have evolved to make use of a process called evaporative cooling. When water evaporates (such as the sweat drying off our skin), it takes heat away with it. This is because, for water to change state from a liquid to a gas, energy is needed. Heat is a type of energy, so as the water evaporates into a gas it takes away some of the heat from whatever is around it.

34

Transpiration

What does evaporative cooling have to do with trees and urban heat islands? The answer is that plants are constantly putting moisture into the air through a process called transpiration. They take water up through their roots, carry it through their stems and then release it from their leaves into the air as vapour.

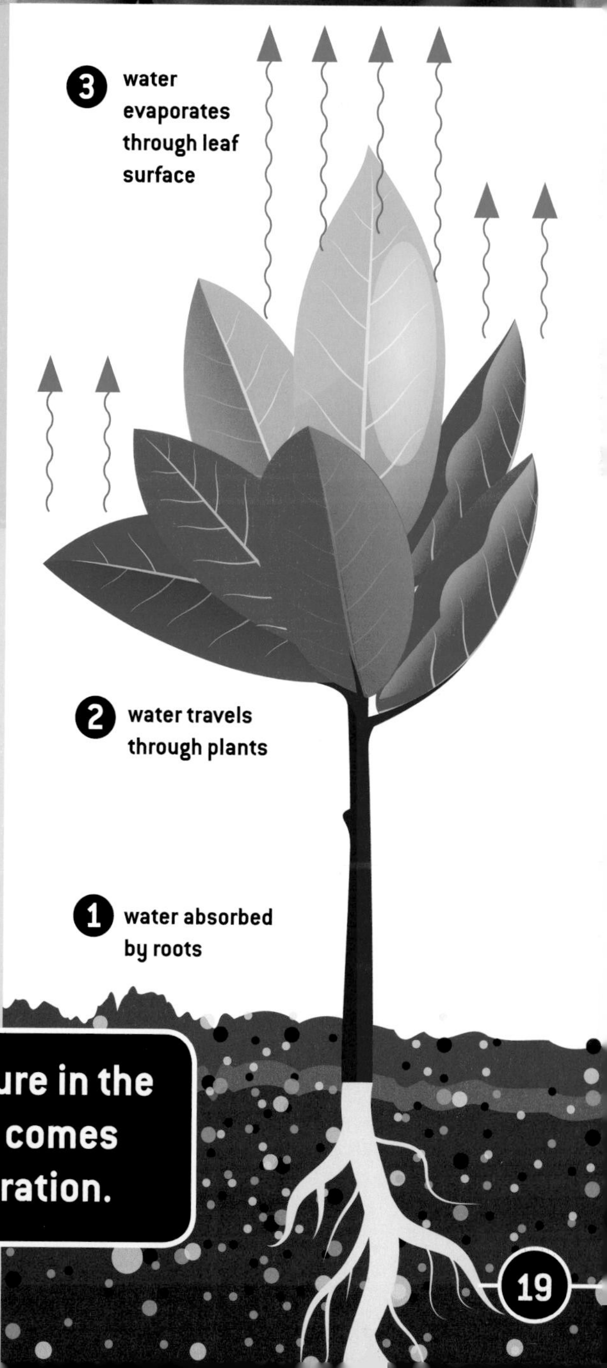
3 water evaporates through leaf surface
2 water travels through plants
1 water absorbed by roots

Cool leaves

This change – from the liquid water inside the plant to the water vapour that is released into the air – needs energy to happen. This energy is taken from the heat in the surrounding air, and so the process of transpiration has a cooling effect on the environment around the plant.

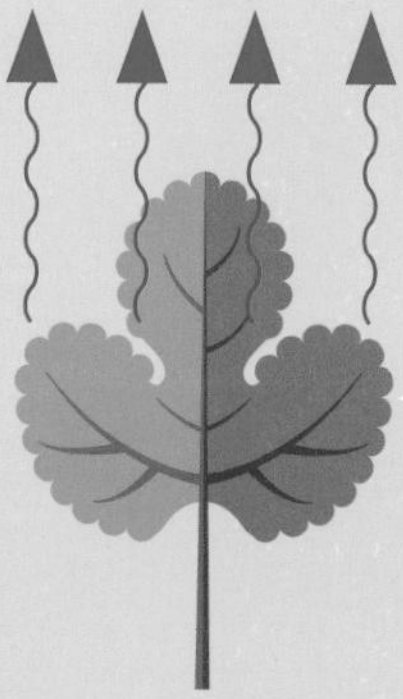

10% of the moisture in the atmosphere comes from transpiration.

SOLVE IT!
COOLING THE CITY

A lack of green space in the city causes three key problems: it makes the city hot, it is bad for people's health, and it stops wildlife from being able to move from place to place. But cities are very tightly packed places and space is at a premium. How can more greenery be added into such crowded areas? Think about the facts below. Can you come up with any solutions?

FACT ONE

Ground space is very valuable in cities, as it is needed for building on.

FACT TWO

Trees can't be planted where buses and cars need to drive, because they would get in the way. But people can walk around and among plants.

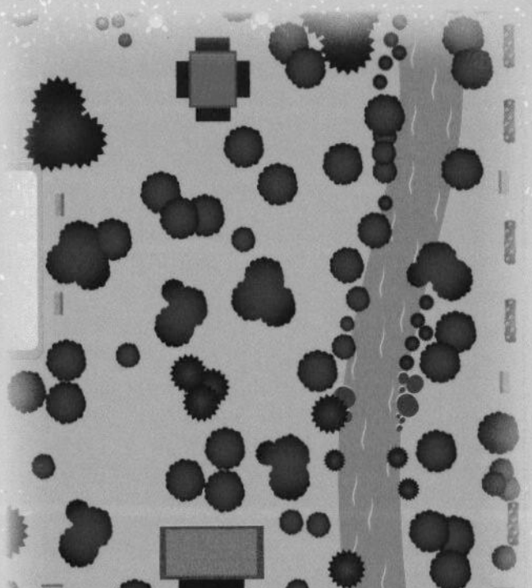

FACT THREE

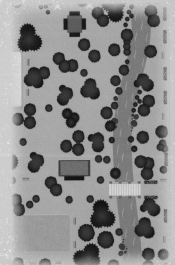

Not all plants need flat ground to grow.

FACT FOUR

Being able to walk or cycle instead of driving is good for people's health.

FACT FIVE

The Sun shines from above, straight onto the top of buildings.

CAN YOU SOLVE IT?

There isn't one 'right' way to add greenery to a city. But smart thinking involves looking at things differently. How can 'dead' space (that is, any space or surface not being productively used) be made more useful?

What exactly are the needs of the people and the wildlife, apart from the cooling effect of the plants on the city overall?

The facts listed here give hints to a couple of different solutions that some cities around the world are already using, but you might also come up with your own brand-new ideas.

Not quite sure? Turn to page 43 to see what some places are already doing.

TEST IT!
THE ALBEDO EFFECT

Study the albedo effect, and how vegetation can reduce it, with this experiment.

YOU WILL NEED

- a sheet of black paper
- a sheet of white paper
- grass clippings or shredded lettuce
- a desk lamp with an incandescent bulb
- a thermometer
- a timer
- a pencil and notebook

STEP 1

Set up your desk lamp so that it is shining directly downwards. Give it a few minutes to heat up. Make sure your lamp has an old-fashioned incandescent bulb, as LED bulbs don't get hot.

STEP 2

Taking care not to touch the bulb, place your white sheet of paper directly under the lamp. Put the thermometer on top of it. Measure the temperature on the thermometer right away, and then every 30 seconds for three minutes. Note down the temperatures.

STEP 3

Remove the white paper and thermometer. Give the thermometer a minute or two to cool down. Now place your black sheet of paper directly under the lamp with the thermometer on top. Record the temperature in the same way.

STEP 4

After you have recorded the temperature every 30 seconds for three minutes, remove the black paper and thermometer. Allow the thermometer to return to room temperature.

STEP 5

Finally, replace the black paper with shredded lettuce or grass clippings, and place the thermometer on top. As they wilt, they'll give off water vapour, mimicking the effect of transpiration. Record the temperature as before.

STEP 6

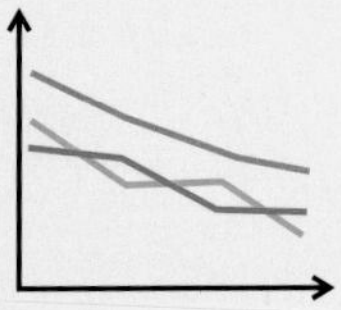

Once you have the temperature data for all three surfaces, plot your results on a line graph. What effect did each of the different surfaces have on the temperature readings?

THE ISSUE:
TOO MUCH TRAFFIC

City roads are busy places, full of buses, taxis, cars, lorries and motorbikes. Most of the time the traffic moves slowly, as the sheer number of vehicles means no one is getting anywhere fast. On top of this, in the city centre traffic lights and pedestrian crossings stop the traffic every few hundred metres. Pedestrians on the pavement breathe in vehicle fumes while they wait to cross the road.

Vehicle emissions

The exhaust fumes that cars and other vehicles release into the atmosphere are very damaging for people and the environment. Globally, road transport produces 16 per cent of the carbon dioxide emissions that are contributing to climate change, but CO_2 isn't the only harmful gas that engines burning petrol or diesel put out. Carbon monoxide, nitrogen oxide and several other harmful gases are products of vehicle engines.

SPOTLIGHT: NITROGEN OXIDE

Nitrogen oxide (NOx) is a pollutant that irritates people's lungs.

NO_x

In 2014, air pollution was linked to

500,000

early deaths across Europe.

Slow going

Car travel is not only very polluting; it can be very slow. As many cities are so densely packed, it isn't possible to move around quickly on the roads. In central New York, for example, the average speed of traffic is just 7.6 kilometres per hour.

Wasting energy

Car travel is a very energy-inefficient means of transport. The average weight of a car is around 1,400 kilograms (kg). The average weight of an adult is around 70 kg. So, a car's engine is carrying 20 times the weight of a human, just to move one human around. Even a car carrying five adults is carrying four times the weight of a human, per passenger.

Car vs. bus

A double-decker bus weighing around 11,500 kg can carry around 80 people. So, a full bus carries around two times the weight of a human, per passenger. This makes the amount of fuel burned per person less for bus travel than car travel.

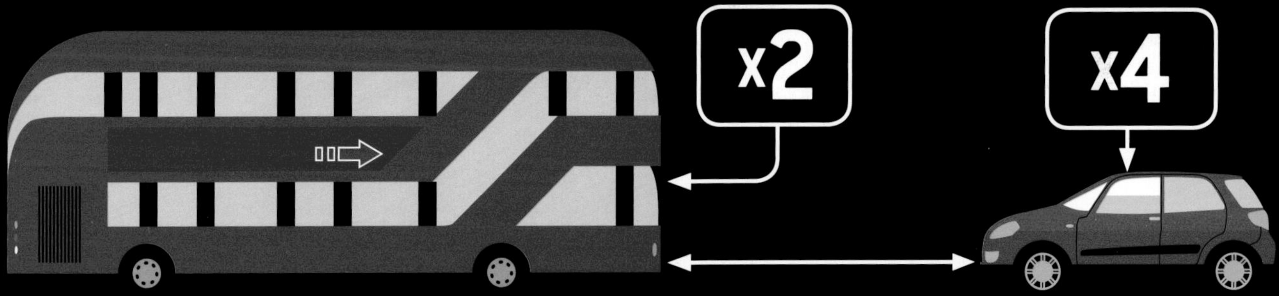

Space on the road

Another way in which car travel is inefficient is space. Compared to a bike, a car takes up a lot of space on the road. One lane on an average road can carry about 2,000 cars per hour, compared with 14,000 bicycles.

TRANSPORT TECHNOLOGY

City transport comes in many forms around the world, each type with different advantages and disadvantages. Here are some of the most widely used types of vehicle technology in cities across the globe.

Car

One key advantage of car travel is the ability to take passengers door to door. Cars can also start their journey at any time, whereas public transport runs on a set schedule. A big disadvantage is that most cars are powered by engines that burn fossil fuels, polluting the air and contributing to climate change. Electric vehicles are becoming more common, but even these eco-friendlier cars have downsides – in crowded cities, heavy traffic makes cars a slow option and it can be difficult to find a place to park.

SPOTLIGHT: ELECTRIC VEHICLES

Powered by rechargeable batteries, electric vehicles contribute less to climate change and air pollution. However, in order to be genuinely environmentally friendly, the electricity must be generated by renewable sources such as the Sun or wind.

Electric cars are cheaper to run than cars that burn fossil fuels.
charging point

Rail or metro

Many cities have underground or overground rail networks. The main advantages of rail technology are speed, capacity (how many people can be transported), safety and environmental impacts. Rail travel is far safer than road travel, and trains can carry hundreds of people very quickly from place to place. The disadvantages are that rail networks are expensive and difficult to build, particularly in places where there are already existing buildings. They also offer fewer stops or routes than road travel.

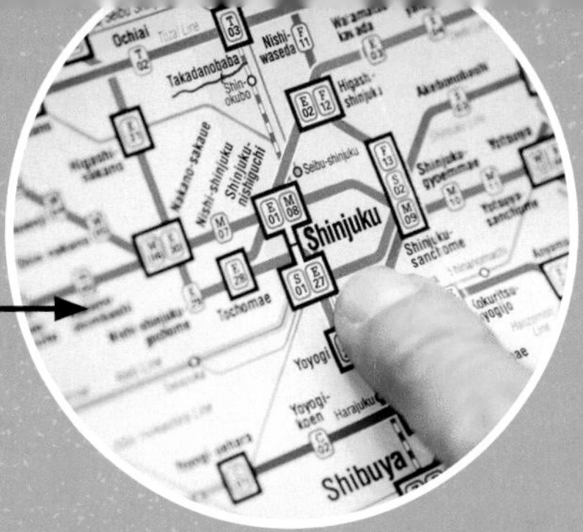

3.33 BILLION
people travel on Tokyo's subway system each year.

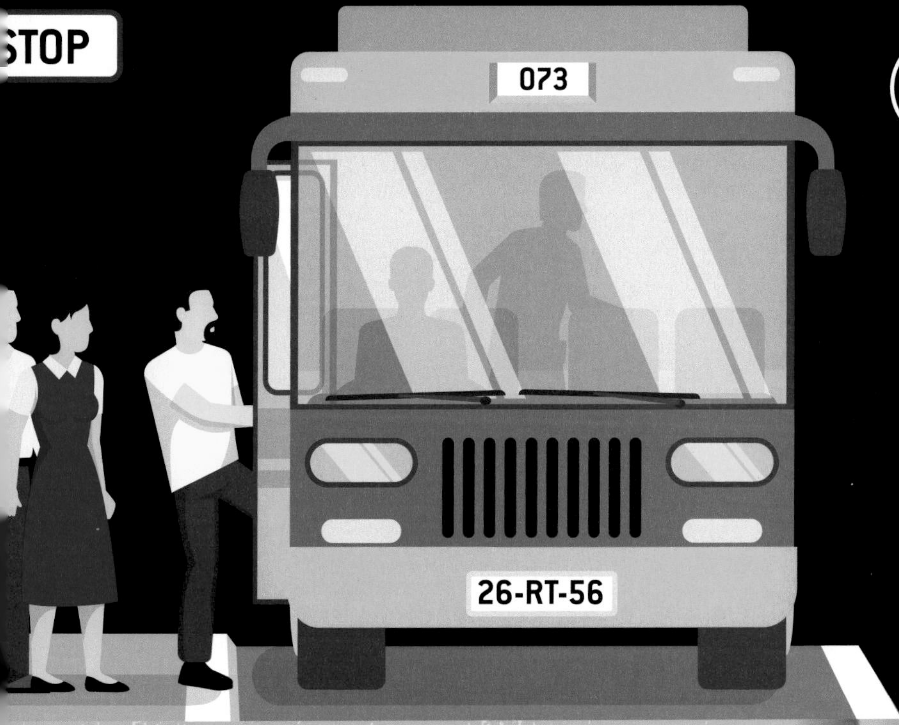

Bus

Buses are more efficient than cars in terms of the energy and space that they use per person. However, unless they are electric they will still contribute to air pollution and carbon emissions. They are slower than rail due to traffic. Although they are less flexible than private vehicles, they can go to more places than rail networks, and new bus routes can be put in place more easily.

Bicycle

The bicycle is the most energy-efficient form of transport. It is space-efficient, flexible and environmentally friendly. However, it uses human power, which can be tiring. When people are forced to share the road with cars and buses, cycling can also be less safe.

SOLVE IT!

INCREASE PUBLIC TRANSPORT

Increasing the number of people who use public transport instead of private cars makes a city more sustainable. But the most efficient types of public transport, such as metro systems, can be difficult to construct in cities that are already very built up. Some cities around the world have installed a system that takes the advantages of different technologies to come up with a new idea. Can you figure out how?

FACT ONE

Many cities were built without a metro or rail system, and so people rely on road transport, causing pollution and delays.

FACT TWO

Cities that rely on road travel often have multi-lane roads (expressways) running through the centre.

FACT THREE

Underground and overground rail systems are fast and efficient because they have a dedicated line (they don't have to compete with other traffic, unlike buses).

FACT FOUR

People buy tickets as they enter the train station. This means they don't have to show tickets as they board, speeding up journey times.

134A

FACT FIVE

Train carriages can carry a lot of people at once. Buses can also carry a lot of people at once.

CAN YOU SOLVE IT?

Consider the facts listed here. Can you think of a way to combine some of the advantages of both bus and train travel to come up with a solution that some cities are already using?

Still a bit stuck? See page 44 for the solution.

TEST IT!

WEIGH YOUR CAR

If your family or a friend's family has a car, try this experiment to figure out how much weight additional to the passengers is being transported when the car is moving.

YOU WILL NEED

a car, plus an adult who can move it
a tyre pressure gauge
a pencil
16 large sheets of thin card
a ruler or measuring tape
a calculator

TIP

A tyre's footprint is roughly square, so wedge a piece of card at the front, back and left and right side of each tyre.

STEP 1

On an area of flat, dry ground, start by measuring the surface area of the bottom on each of the car's four tyres. Do this by wedging sheets of card underneath each tyre as far as you can, on each of the four sides of the tyres.

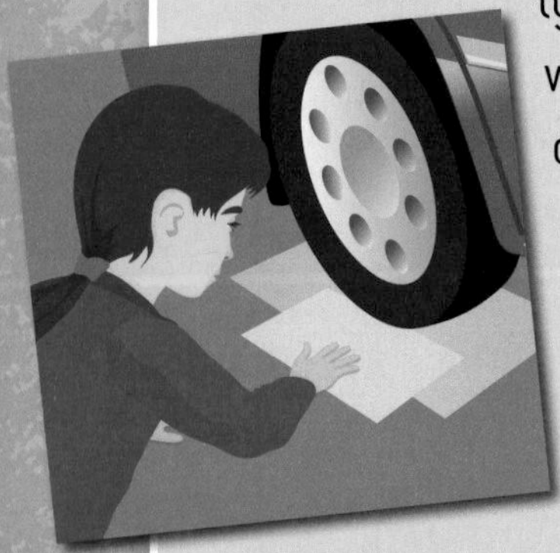

STEP 2

Ask your adult to carefully move the car off the card pieces, and measure the length and width of the empty square in the centre of each set of four card pieces. Multiply the length by the width to find the area in square inches or centimetres. This is the footprint of each tyre.

STEP ③

Ask your adult to measure the air pressure inside each tyre using the pressure gauge. Make sure to note down which tyre measurement is which!

TIP

Most gauges measure in imperial units, with PSI or pounds per square inch. Other gauges give the metric kg/cm². If your gauge uses PSI, measure the footprint in inches too, to make the calculation simpler.

STEP ④

To calculate the weight each tyre is holding up, multiply the tyre's surface area by the air-pressure reading for that tyre. The number you are left with is the weight, for example:

38 square inches x 34 PSI = 1,292 pounds

Add the weight carried by all four tyres together to get the weight of the car.

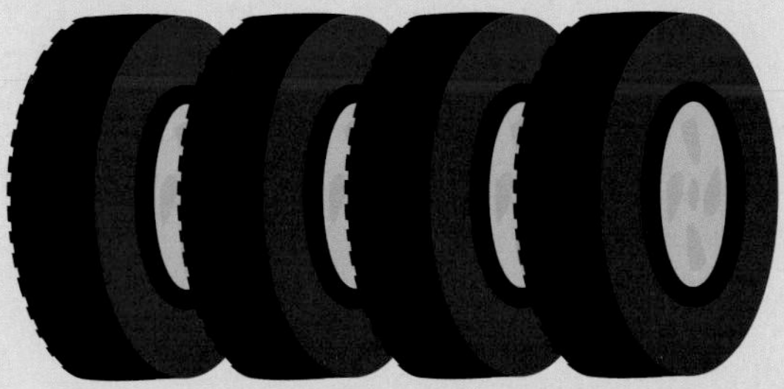

ADD TOGETHER ALL FOUR TYRES

SPOTLIGHT:

TYRE PRESSURES

Car tyres are designed to be used at a specific air pressure. An under-inflated tyre will wear out quickly, increase the fuel consumption of the vehicle and make it dangerous to drive.

THE ISSUE:

LIGHT POLLUTION

The sky glow of Los Angeles in the USA can be seen from a plane

320 km away.

The dazzling and multi-coloured lights that illuminate streets, billboards and buildings are part of a city's identity and attraction. There are even songs about the 'bright lights' of the city. Electric lighting is an important technology that allows us to do all sorts of things. But the large amount of unnecessary artificial light shining out into the night sky is having negative effects on wildlife and people – and it's getting worse each year.

Wildlife

Animals have adapted over millions of years to the pattern of night and day, and for many animals, darkness at night is very important. Many birds use the stars to help them find their way when they are migrating. However, the amount of artificial light put into the night sky can cause these birds to become lost and unable to reach their feeding or breeding grounds.

Only 1 in 1,000 hatchlings survive, due to disorientation, habitat destruction and natural predators.

SPOTLIGHT: TURTLES

Baby sea turtles find their way to the sea by heading away from the dark shadows created by sand dunes. But the lights of coastal cities confuse them, and many head in to the city instead where they get run over or stuck in drains.

Human health

It isn't just animals who are affected – light pollution is bad for humans too. Our body knows when to go to sleep and when to wake up, thanks to hormones we produce when it is dark. Artificial lighting can confuse our natural body clock, meaning we don't get enough sleep, making it hard to concentrate and weakening our immune systems.

Waste of energy

Another issue with light pollution is that it is a waste of energy. Lighting is powered by electricity. So if a lot of the light is being lost to the night sky, it is wasted energy. Even though modern LED lights are more energy-efficient, this often encourages cities to just install more of them, rather than reducing the amount of light being wasted.

Light pollution at night across Europe, seen from space

UNDERSTANDING LIGHT

Light is incredibly important to humans. We use it to see, and our entire existence depends on it, since plants create food using sunlight, which then ultimately provides the food for all the other living things on Earth. But what is light, and how does it behave?

Energy

Light is a kind of energy. Energy is the ability to do work – it's what makes things happen. There are lots of different forms of energy, such as chemical energy or electrical energy. Energy can be changed between forms. For example, the process of photosynthesis, which plants use to make food, changes light energy into chemical energy. Solar panels (right) change light energy into electrical energy.

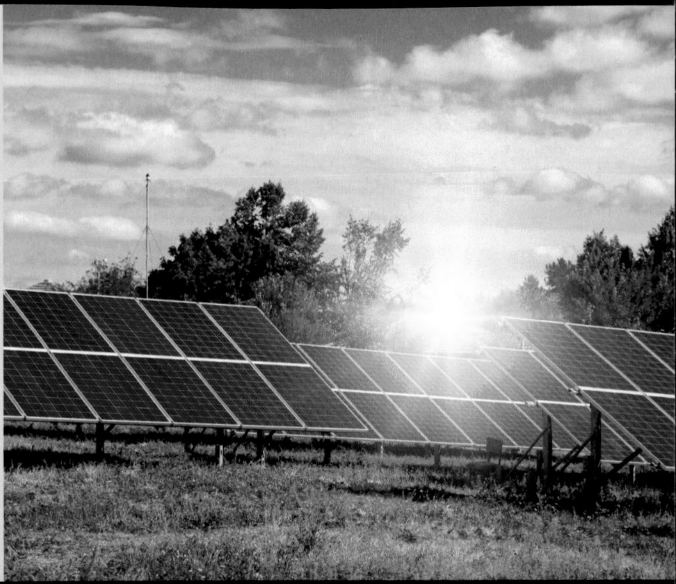

Light is made of waves and always travels in straight lines called rays. However, the direction in which light moves can be affected in a few key ways:

1 Reflection

One of the most obvious effects is reflection. When light hits a surface, it bounces back. This effect can be seen very clearly with a shiny surface such as a mirror. However, even dull surfaces reflect some light. The light bouncing off objects and entering our eyes is how we see them.

2 Refraction

When light moves between materials, for example from air into water, it refracts. This is a bending of the light ray at the boundary point between the materials. This is what causes drinking straws in water glasses to appear bent or broken.

SPOTLIGHT:

VISIBLE LIGHT

Birds can see more colours of light than we can. They can see ultraviolet light, which is invisible to human eyes.

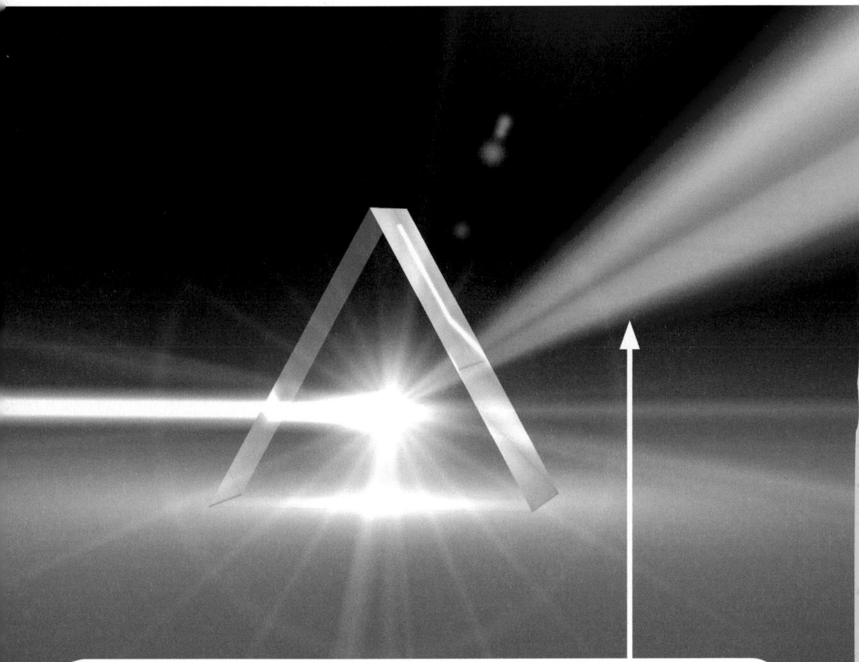

3 Dispersion

White light is actually made up of all the colours of the rainbow, blended together. You can split a beam of white light into different colours if you shine it through a prism. This is called dispersion. This happens because the different colours have very slightly different wavelengths, which are refracted by the prism in very slightly different amounts.

Colours of light

Light that looks white can contain more of one colour. For example, daylight that comes from the Sun contains more blue light than light from a candle, which contains more yellow light. Most LED bulbs give off more blue light than old-fashioned incandescent light bulbs, although LEDs with a 'warm' yellow colour are also available. Because blue artificial light more closely resembles daylight, it contributes more to light pollution than yellow light.

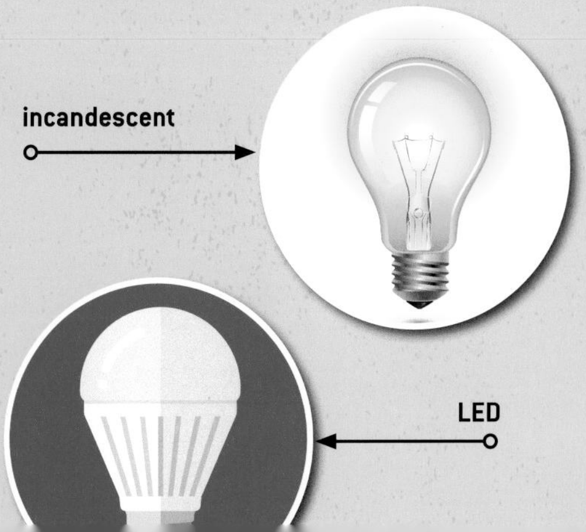

SOLVE IT!

REDUCE LIGHT POLLUTION

Reversing the trend of light pollution would be better for human health, helpful to wildlife, and would save energy. However, cities do need lighting to keep streets safe and accessible in the evening. Can you come up with any ways to reduce the problem of light pollution while still keeping streets lit? Look at the scenes below and consider what changes could be made.

SCENE ONE

Look at the street lights running alongside the river. What do you notice about their design? How could they be designed differently?

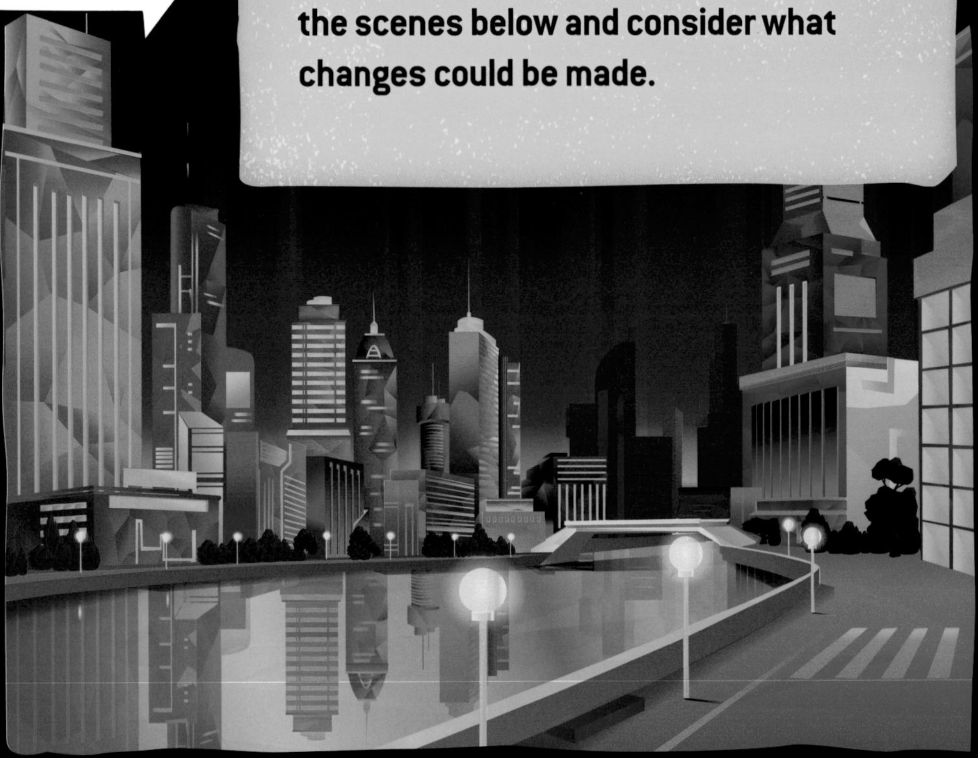

SCENE TWO

Consider the overly bright outdoor lighting on this house. What changes could the owners make?

SCENE THREE

These city park lights are on at all times. Could technology be used to reduce the effect on the local wildlife?

SCENE FOUR

Very bright, blue-tinted LEDs have been installed around this bus stop. What other options are there for lighting it up?

CAN YOU SOLVE IT?

Taking into account what you know about light and light pollution, come up with ways that light pollution could be reduced in each of these four scenes. There may be more than one solution for each, but try and come up with four different ideas.

Need some help? See page 45 for some possible solutions.

TEST IT! STREET LIGHT DESIGN

In this experiment, try out some different street light designs to see which causes the least light pollution.

YOU WILL NEED

two small lights, such as E10 bulbs with socket, wires and batteries, or a couple of small pen-style torches with the reflector removed

sticky tack

pipe cleaners

electrical tape

scissors

a small cardboard box

aluminium foil

one or two small figurines

a dark room

STEP 1

First create a starry sky by making a planetarium with your small cardboard box. Make a hole just big enough to fit your light bulb in on the underside, and several small pin holes on the top side. Cover any other cracks or gaps in the box with electrical tape. When you switch the bulb inside the box on in a dark room, it should project little dots of 'starlight' onto the ceiling.

STEP 2

Create your street light. If you have a pen torch with the reflector taken off, you can simply stand the torch on its end (with sticky tack to secure it if necessary), and the body of the torch will act as the lamp post, with the light at the top.

STEP 3

If you have a small bulb in a socket, you'll need to create a post to hold it up using pipe cleaners. Twist several together to make a strong post. Hook the bulb onto the top of the post. With pipe cleaners you have the option to angle the bulb sideways or down towards the table.

STEP 4

In a dark room, place both your planetarium light and your street light on a table. Add the figurines below the street light. Turn both lights on. With your street light unshielded, it should wash out the small pin pricks of starlight on the ceiling.

STEP 5

Next, try making lamp shades in various designs to sit over the bulb of your street lamp using the aluminium foil. Can you create a design that effectively lights up the figurines in the 'street', but allows the 'stars' to be visible in the sky above?

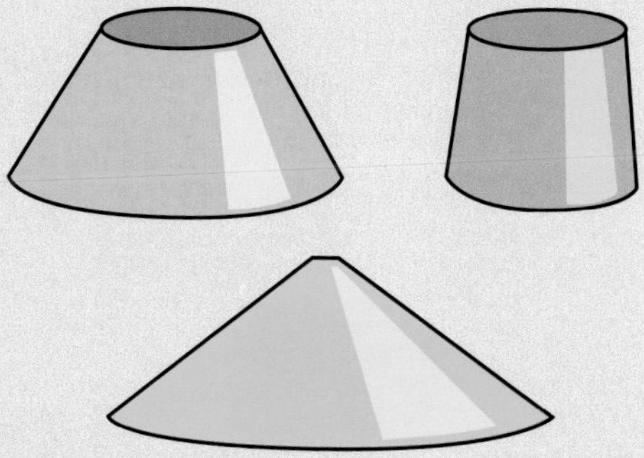

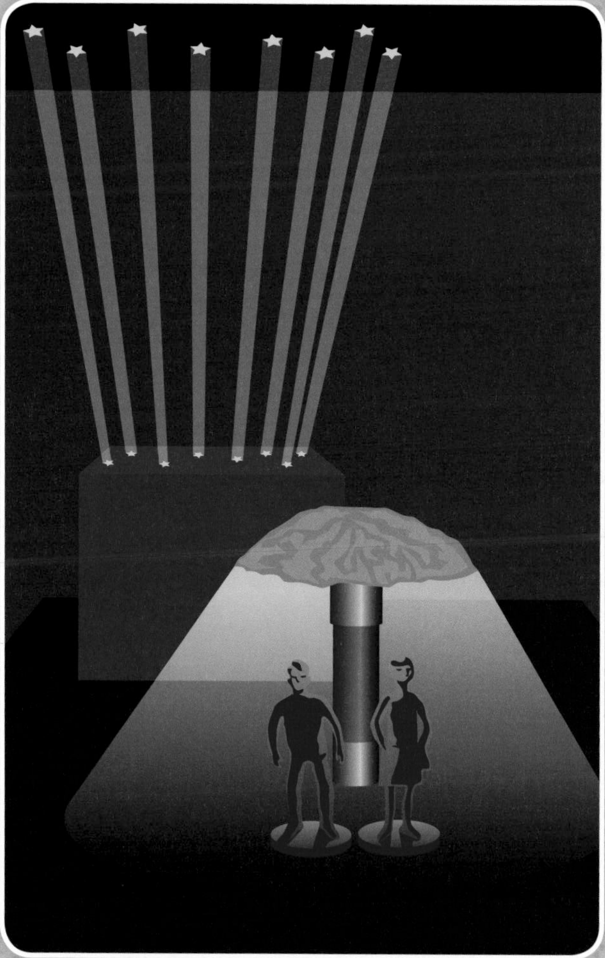

CITIES IN THE FUTURE

The way many of our cities look now, with super-high gleaming skyscrapers and modern forms of transport, would have been unimaginable to people a century ago. It's likely that the way many of our cities look in 50 to 100 years will be radically different again. Here are some far-out ideas, and some projects that scientists, engineers and architects are working on right now.

Sky forests

The Bosco Verticale (Vertical Forest) in Milan, Italy, is a pair of apartment blocks covered in trees. It is one of the first developments to reforest an area by building new homes! If the same amount of trees were grown on flat land, they would take up an area of 20,000 square metres, around the size of three football pitches. The trees help cool the city, clean the air and improve biodiversity.

The Bosco Verticale in Milan, Italy

SPOTLIGHT:

ECO CITY

An eco city is an entire city that has been designed to be completely environmentally friendly, by producing no carbon emissions and recycling water and waste. The governments of China and Singapore are currently working together to develop an eco city 40 km from Tianjin city in China.

Cycle through the air

Cycling is the most eco-friendly type of transport apart from walking, but it can be hard work, you can get wet in the rain and other traffic can make it less safe. Enter the idea of enclosed cycle lanes running through the air. The air in these tunnels could be circulated so that cyclists always have the wind at their backs, reducing the effort of cycling by up to 90 per cent.

A covered cycle lane in Glasgow

Floating cities

With a growing global population and the threat of sea level rise due to climate change, designers have begun to develop ideas for cities that would float on the sea. These high-tech ocean settlements would contain everything the citizens needed, including farms, housing, schools, offices and hospitals, and would be powered by renewable sources such as solar energy.

Glowing trees

Bioluminescence is the ability some living things – such as fireflies, some jellyfish, and even some fungi – have to give off light. Scientists are working out how to genetically engineer whole trees so that they have the same ability. These trees could then be used as a sustainable form of low-level street lighting!

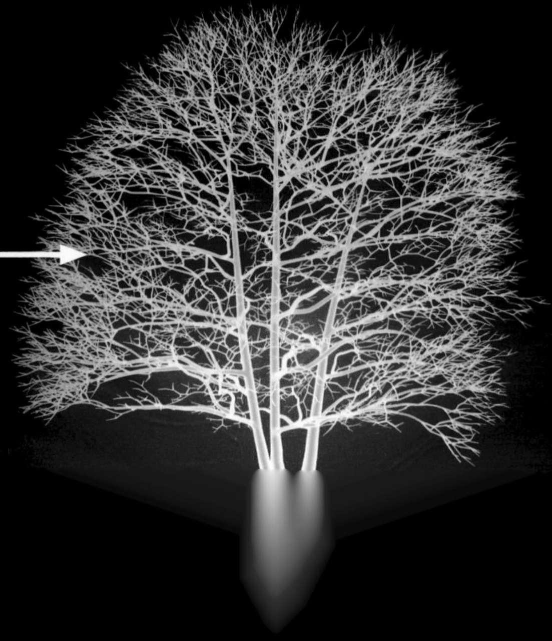

ANSWERS

SOLVE IT! SUSTAINABLE CITY PLANNING PAGES 12–13

Every new city needs to take into account the unique features of where it is being built. However, there are certain general principles that make new cities more sustainable, including the following:

TRANSPORT

Where possible, people should be encouraged to walk or cycle by providing wide, safe pathways and cycle lanes. For longer routes, public transport networks should be built.

HOUSING

High-density options such as apartment blocks are better, as they can accommodate a lot of people on a small patch of land.

Your map and picture

You can probably come up with lots of different designs and ideas for your bird's-eye view and street view. If you would like some more inspiration, why not search for 'eco city' online to see what designs architects have already created.

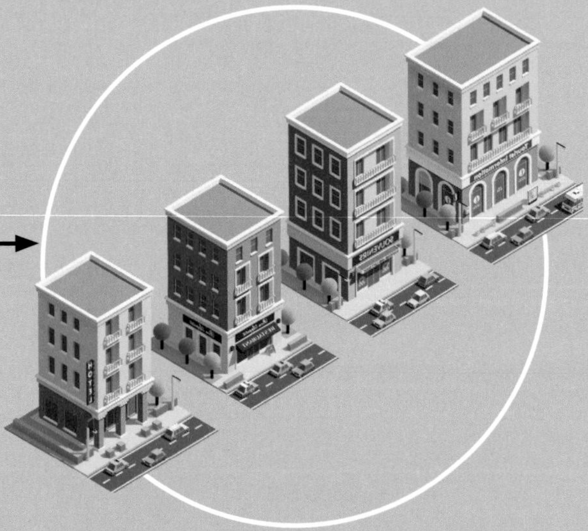

FACILITIES

All the facilities that people need should be built among the housing, for example using the ground floor of an apartment block as a library, and the top floor as a health clinic. By keeping shops, offices, schools and housing all close together, this ensures that people can walk to where they need to go, and helps maintain a sense of community in the city.

SOLVE IT! COOLING THE CITY PAGES 20–21

Adding green space to a city to help reduce the heat island effect can be done in lots of different ways, and has the added benefits of making people happier and helping wildlife to thrive. Here are some design solutions:

Green roofs

Often the tops of buildings in cities are unused, dead space. Some architects have started designing buildings to include 'green roofs' that are covered in vegetation, such as these in Sydney, Australia. As well as the cooling effect and the positive impacts on people and wildlife, they bring design advantages, such as absorbing rainwater and insulating the building.

Living walls

Not all plants need to grow on flat ground. Why not cover the walls of a building with vegetation, like this building in Paris, France? They make use of otherwise unused vertical wall space, are good for wildlife and the environment and look cool too.

Green ways

Long thin trails or parks that run through a city are called green ways. This is an aerial green way called the High Line in New York, USA. They can often be installed along old railway routes or canal tow paths. Connected green corridors that run through cities can help wildlife move to new habitats and are a great place for people to exercise and relax.

ANSWERS

SOLVE IT! INCREASE PUBLIC TRANSPORT PAGES 28–29

An innovative type of public transport that includes some of the advantages of a metro system but can make use of the existing road system is called a bus rapid transit, or BRT system. These are already used in a lot of cities in Central and South America and in other countries too. You may have come up with a similar idea:

A BRT system gives over certain lanes in existing roads to special buses which have several carriages, like a metro train. They only stop to let people on at specified stops, which are enclosed. This means tickets must be purchased in order to enter the stops, making boarding speedy.

Like the metro, a BRT system can carry a lot of people, and because the buses are given their own lane and priority at junctions, they don't have to compete with traffic. The best BRT systems use electric vehicles to reduce air pollution, too.

The world's largest BRT network is in Jakarta in Indonesia. It covers 230.9 kilometres of road in the city.

SOLVE IT!

REDUCE LIGHT POLLUTION PAGES 36–37

When it comes to reducing light pollution, the questions to ask are: could the design be better, could we use less light and could we use a different type of light? The examples shown could have more than one solution, but here are a few key suggestions.

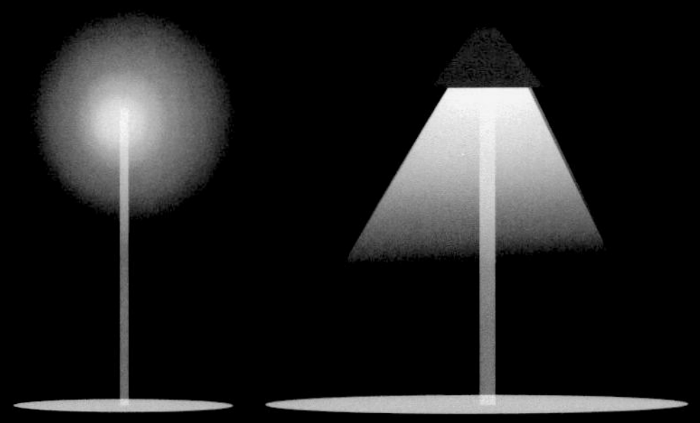

Scene one

The lights in scene one send light in all directions, including towards the sky where it isn't needed. A different design of lamp shade could direct the light only downwards where it is useful.

Scene two

In scene two the lights are unnecessarily bright. Lights with a motion sensor and less powerful, lower wattage could be used, while still providing enough light to let people walk around safely.

Scene three

The lights in scene three are on all night, disturbing the wildlife. If there are no people around, the light is unnecessary. Smart sensors could be used so that lights only come on when people are walking around.

Scene four

In scene four, the blue-tinted LED lights could be swapped for LEDs with a yellow or red tint. Blue light is more like daylight, so the effects on human health and wildlife are stronger. Avoiding using blue-tinted lights can reduce harm.

MAKING A DIFFERENCE

Although some of the key ideas about how to make cities more sustainable in this book can't be acheived by any one person alone, there are things we can all do to move in the right direction.

Choose your transport

Always walk, cycle or take public transport if you can. Walking and cycling are the most eco-friendly types of transport if your destination is close enough, but public transport is better than getting a lift in a car for longer journeys. Encourage your family members to do the same, as it's better for everyone's health, too!

Green your windowsill

You might not be able to plant trees on your roof or cover the walls of the building you live in with plants, but you can get a window box and grow some greenery there. Flowers will provide food for insects, and the greenery will cheer up people who see your home from the street.

THINK BIG!

Are there any ways that you think your city could be more environmentally friendly that aren't listed in this book? Try and come up with some big **STEAM** ideas for ways we can all live better in an urban landscape.

GLOSSARY

albedo effect the process by which light-coloured surfaces reflect more heat than dark-coloured surfaces

architect someone whose job it is to design buildings

biodiversity the variety of different plants and animals in an area

Burgess Model a city or town layout planned in concentric, or bigger and bigger, circles with the most expensive land and buildings in the centre

city planning deciding how to organise a city and use the land, including where to have parks, hospitals, schools and other important buildings

climate change a change in weather patterns and temperatures around the world, caused by human activity

emissions something that has been released or put out into the world, such as gases coming out of a car exhaust

facilities places, services or pieces of equipment that have a particular purpose – for example, schools, shops and public toilets

fossil fuel a fuel such as oil, coal or gas that was formed over millions of years from dead plants and animals

green belt an area of open land around a city, where building is not allowed or limited

greenery growing plants that have green leaves

greenhouse gas a gas in our atmosphere that traps the heat from the Sun, contributing to climate change

habitat fragmentation where an animal or plant's natural environment is split up into smaller separate pieces as a result of human development or environmental changes

infrastructure the basic systems, such as roads, electricity supply and sewage, that are necessary for daily life to go on

LED bulb a type of lightbulb that uses much less energy than an old-fashioned lightbulb – LED stands for 'light-emitting diode'

light pollution brightening of the night sky caused by light from houses and street lamps

megacity a huge city in which more than 10 million people live

migrate to move from one area to another at different times of the year

photosynthesis the process by which plants make food for themselves using water, carbon dioxide and energy from the Sun

pollution the presence in the environment of objects or substances that are harmful

population density the number of people living in a certain amount of space (usually measured in people per square kilometre)

recreational to do with free time and relaxing or having fun

rural describing the countryside, as opposed to a town or city

suburbs areas on the edge of a city or large town where housing is more spread out

sustainable when something can be maintained at the same level for a very long time because it doesn't harm the environment or use up limited natural resources

transpiration the process by which plants take up water from the soil and release it as water vapour into the air

urbanisation an increase in the proportion of people living in urban areas compared to rural areas

urban sprawl when a city or large town grows and spreads out into the surrounding countryside

INDEX

ECO STEAM TITLES IN THE SERIES

the CITIES WE LIVE IN

City life
Eco-freindly cities
THE ISSUE: Urban sprawl
Urban land use
Solve it! Sustainable city planning
Test it! Land use project
THE ISSUE: Lack of green space
Heating and cooling
Solve it! Cool the city
Test it! The albedo effect
THE ISSUE: Too much traffic
Transport technology
Solve it! Increase public transport
Test it! Weigh your car
THE ISSUE: Light pollution
Understanding light
Solve it! Reduce light pollution
Test it! Street light design
Cities in the future

the CROPS WE GROW

Farming around the world
Impacts of farming
THE ISSUE: Rainforest deforestation
Habitat destruction
Solve it! Farm without deforestation
Test it! Mixed-veg garden project
THE ISSUE: Soil erosion
What is soil?
Solve it! Protect the soil
Test it! Soil erosion experiment
THE ISSUE: Pollinators under threat
Plants, pollinators and ecosystems
Solve it! Pollinator-friendly farming
Test it! Pollinator survey
THE ISSUE: Lost plant variety
Evolution and inheritance
Solve it! Climate-proof farming
Test it! Heritage varieties
Farming in the future

the ENERGY WE USE

Understanding energy
How we use fuels
THE ISSUE: Climate change
Producing power
Solve it! Green energy sources
Test it! Build a mini-wind turbine
THE ISSUE: Running out of oil
Alternative fuels
Solve it! Fuel from waste
Test it! Biogas experiment
THE ISSUE: Pollution in the air
What happens when fuels burn?
Solve it! Power a vehicle
Test it! Make a mini-solar car
THE ISSUE: Energy demand
Battery technology
Solve it! 24 hour-power
Test it! Solar heater experiment
The future of power

the FOOD WE EAT

Food, waste and climate change
The big issues
THE ISSUE: Animal farming impacts
Diet and nutrition
Solve it! Design a balanced menu
Test it! Make bean burgers
THE ISSUE: Overfishing
Food chains and ecosystems
Solve it! Sustainable fish farming
Test it! Grow lettuces in water
THE ISSUE: Problems with packaging
Properties of plastics
Solve it! Preventing plastic pollution
Test it! Make corn plastic
THE ISSUE: Food waste
Decomposition
Solve it! Waste-free sugar
Test it! Make your own compost
Food in the futureIndex

the HOUSES WE BUILD

The technology of building
Impacts of construction
THE ISSUE: A concrete problem
Sustainable materials
Solve it! Design eco-homes
Test it! Make a brick
THE ISSUE: Energy-hungry homes
The Earth's tilt
Solve it! Using the Sun's energy
Test it! Sunlight and the seasons
THE ISSUE: Too hot or too cold
Thermal energy transfers
Solve it! Prevent heat loss
Test it! Insulation experiment
THE ISSUE: Unsustainable water use
The water cycle
Solve it! Reduce water consumption
Test it! Make a water filter
Houses in the future

the STUFF WE BUY

Material World
Making things, making waste
THE ISSUE: Throwaway fashion
How fabric is made
Solve It! Cotton alternatives
Test it! Upcycled clothing
THE ISSUE: Polluting paper
Product manufacturing
Solve it! Stop wasting resources
Test it! Handmade paper
THE ISSUE: Waste electronics
What is circular design?
Solve it! A new system
Test it! Make a toy
THE ISSUE: Too much stuff
How we use things
Solve it! Saving and sharing
Test it! Build a sharing website
The future of making